MILITARY AIRCRAFT OF THE WORLD

Hiroshi Seo

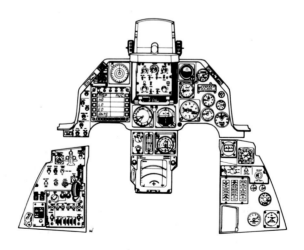

First published in Japan in 1979 by
Yama-Kei Publishers Co Ltd, Tokyo

Photographs © Hiroshi Seo, 1979

Text © Jane's Publishing Co Ltd, 1981

First published in Great Britain in 1981 by
Jane's Publishing Company Ltd
238 City Road, London EC1V 2PU

Distributed in Canada, the Philippines
and the USA and its dependencies by
Science Book International, Inc
51 Sleeper Street
Boston, Massachusetts MA 02210

ISBN 0 86720 559 8

Printed in Japan

Front Cover: General Dynamics F-16
Back Cover: Vought A-7 Corsair II

JANE'S

Contents

Grumman F-14 Tomcat (USA, 1970): US Navy's carrier-borne multi-purpose fighter with long-range radar system and Phoenix missiles. Automatically controlled swing-wing system provides outstanding manoeuvrability. *Span:* 19.54–10.15 m (64 ft 1½ in–38 ft 2½ in) *Length:* 18.90 m (61 ft 11¾ in) *Max speed:* Mach 2.34 *Powerplant:* 2 × Pratt & Whitney TF30-P-412A turbofans, each 9,500 kg (20,900 lb) st with afterburning

F-14A at NAS Oceana (US Navy), August 1978
300 mm KM f5.6 + ½ 1/250

McDonnell Douglas F-15 Eagle (USA, 1972): Air superiority fighter. Thrust–weight ratio of nearly 2 to 1 makes the Eagle highly manoeuvrable. *Span:* 13.05 m (42ft 9¾ in) *Length:* 19.43 m (63 ft 9 in) *Max speed:* Mach 2.5 *Powerplant:* 2 × Pratt & Whitney F100-PW-100 turbofans, each 11,340 kg (24,000 lb) st with afterburning

F-15A at Bitburg AB (West Germany, USAFE), May 1978 28 mm KM f5.6 + ½ 1/250

5

McDonnell Douglas F-18 Hornet (USA, 1978): Naval strike fighter for 1980's, assisting F-14 and replacing F-4 and Corsair II (A-7). Fitted with small but high-performance radar weapon system APG-65. *Span:* 11.43 m (37 ft 6 in) *Length:* 17.07 m (56 ft 0 in) *Max speed:* Mach 1.8 *Powerplant:* 2 × GE F404-GE-400 turbofans, each, 7,257 kg (16,000 lb) st

F-18A at McDonnell Douglas Corp., St. Louis, Mo., USA, September 1978
300 mm KM f8 + ½ 1/250

General Dynamics F-16 Fighting Falcon (USA, 1974): Lightweight combat fighter in production for four NATO air forces and complementing main USAF fighter F-15. F-16B is two-seat trainer version. *Span:* 9.45 m (31 ft 0 in) *Length:* 14.52 m (47 ft 7½ in) *Max speed:* Mach 1.95 *Powerplant:* 1 × Pratt & Whitney F-100-PW-100 turbofan, 11,340 kg (25,000 lb) st with a/b

F-16B at Hill AFB (USAF), March 1979
300 mm KM f5.6 1/500

Northrop F-5E Tiger II (USA, 1972): Single-seat lightweight tactical fighter, development of F5A Freedom Fighter. The F-5E has been optimised for interceptor role. *Span:* 8.13 m (26 ft 8 in) *Length:* 14.68 m (48 ft 2 in) *Max speed:* Mach 1.6 *Powerplant:* 2 × General Electric J85-GE-21A turbojets, each 2,267 kg (5,000 lb) st with afterburning

F-5E at NAS Oceana (US Navy), August 1978 200 mm KMf4 + ⅓ 1/500

McDonnell Douglas F-4 Phantom II (USA, 1958): Tactical strike fighter with large combat load capability and high performance manoeuvrability. Total production over 5,000 and many variants. *Span:* 11.76 m (38 ft 5 in) *Length:* 18.60 m (62 ft 11¾ in) *Max speed:* Mach 2.4 *Powerplant:* 2 × General Electric J79-GE17 turbojets, each 8,120 kg (17,900 lb) st with a/b

Phantom FGR.2 in Air Tattoo (UK), June 1979
400 mm KR f5.6 1/500

9

General Dynamics F-111 (USA, 1964): Tactical strike fighter-bomber with large combat load (7,250 kg) capability. World's first swing-wing aircraft to enter service. Production ended 1973. *Span:* 19.20–9.74 m (63 ft 0 in–31 ft 11½ in)

Length: 22.40 m (73 ft 6 in) *Max speed:* Mach 2.5 *Powerplant:* 2 × Pratt & Whitney turbofans, each 8,390 kg (18,500 lb) st with a/b

F-111F at RAF Lakenheath (UK), June 1979
KR f4 + ⅔ 1/500

General Dynamics (Convair) F-106 Delta Dart (USA, 1956): All-weather interceptor. Somewhat elderly delta-wing fighter (flew first trials on 26 December, 1956). Front-line service with Aerospace Defence Command, still in operation. *Span:* 11.67 m (38 ft 3½ in) *Length:* 21.56 m (70 ft 8¾ in) *Max speed:* Mach 2.3 *Powerplant:* 1 × Pratt & Whitney J75-P-17 turbojet, 11,113 kg (24,500 lb) st with afterburning

F-106A after take-off from Fresno Airport, Calif., March 1979 1979 28 mm KM f5.6 + ⅓ 1/250

Fairchild (Republic) F-105 Thunderchief (USA, 1955): Long-range fighter-bomber produced from mid 1950's to early 1960's. Was used extensively in Vietnam; after front-line withdrawal has been issued to Air National Guard wings. *Span:* 10.65 m (34 ft 11 in) *Length:* 19.62 m (67 ft 0¼ in) *Max speed:* Mach 2.03 *Powerplant:* 1 × Pratt & Whitney J75-P-19W turbojet, 12,030 kg (26,500 lb) st with afterburning

F-105D after take-off from McConnell AFB (USAF), March 1979

28 mm KM f5.6 1/250

Lockheed F-104 Starfighter (USA, 1954): Interceptor, all-weather strike-fighter. Unlike swept-wing contemporaries, built with needle-like fuselage and very thin straight wings. Large numbers built and widely exported. *Span:* 6.69 m (21 ft 11 in)

Length: 16.68 m (54 ft 9 in) *Max speed:* Mach 2.0 *Powerplant:* 1 × General Electric J79-GE-19 turbojet, 8,120 kg (17,900 lb) st with afterburning

CF-104s at Abbotsford Air Show, Canada, August 1977
300 mm KR f5.6+2/3 1/500

13

Fairchild A-10 Thunderbolt II (USA, 1972): Close-support attack aircraft with combined total capacity of 8,400 kg (3 external pylons under fuselage and 4 under each wing). 30 mm GAU-8/A rotary cannon designed to destroy tanks. *Span:* 17.53 m (57 ft 6 in) *Length:* 16.26 m (53 ft 4 in) *Max speed:* 722 km/h (500 mph) *Powerplant:* 2 × General Electric TF34-GE-100 turbofans, each 4,112 kg (9,065 lb) st

A-10A at RAF Bentwaters (UK), June 1979

50 mm KM f8 1/250

Vought A-7 Corsair II (USA, 1965): Tactical carrier-borne attack aircraft, succeeding A-4 Skyhawk. Two external weapon stations on fuselage and 6 underwing pylons carry maximum combined load of 6,800 kg (15,000 lb) including AAMs. *Span:* 11.80 m (38 ft 9 in) *Length:* 14.06 m (46 ft 1½ in) Mach 0.97 *Powerplant:* 1 × Allison TF41-A-1, 6,465 kg (14,250 lb) st

USAF A-7D shot from KC-135 tanker, March 1979
28 mm KM f5.6 1/250

15

Grumman A-6 Intruder (USA, 1960): Carrier-borne low-level strike aircraft. Comparatively slow but has maximum capacity of 6,800 kg (15,000 lb) and an advanced onboard computer with multi-mode radar. *Span:* 16.15 m (53 ft 0 in) *Length:* 16.64 m (54 ft 7 in) *Max speed:* Mach 0.86 *Powerplant:* 2 × Pratt & Whitney J52-P-8A turbojets, each 4,218 kg (9,300 lb) st *A-6E after take-off from NAS Oceana (US Navy), August 1978 300 mm KR f5.6 + ⅓ 1/500*

McDonnell Douglas A-4 Skyhawk (USA, 1954): Carrier or land-based attack bomber. Although small has combined maximum weapon capacity of 4,150 kg. In production for 25 years. *Span:* 8.38 (27 ft 6 in) *Length:* 12.27 m (40 ft 3½ in) *Max speed:* Mach 0.94 *Powerplant:* 1 × Pratt & Whitney J52-P-408A turbojet, 5,080 kg (11,200 lb) st

A-4Fs after take-off from NAS El Centro (US Navy), August 1978

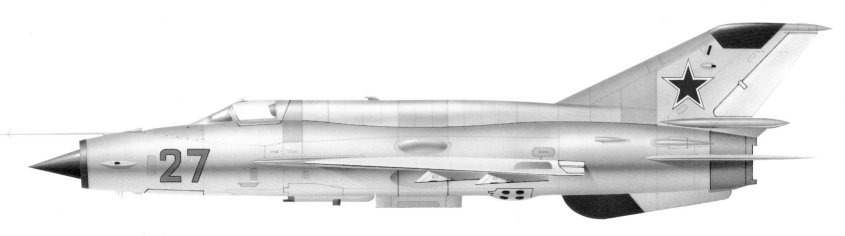

Mikoyan MiG-21 *Fishbed* (USSR, 1955): Multi-purpose fighter and the most widely used by Eastern bloc countries. First flown in 1955, still in production. Good manoeuvrability but radar and armament now outclassed. *Span:* 7.15 m (23 ft 5½ in) *Length:* 15.76 m (51 ft 8½ in) *Max speed:* Mach 2.1 *Powerplant:* 1 × Tumansky R-13-30 turbojet, 6,600 kg (14,500 lb) st

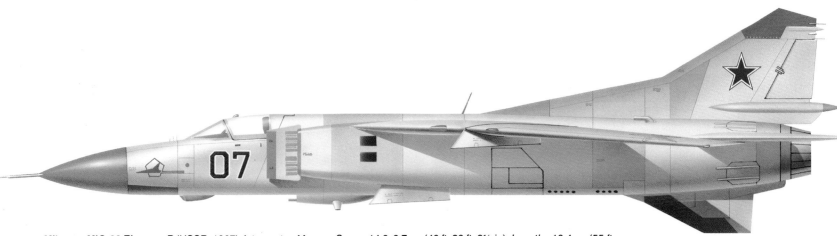

Mikoyan MiG-23 *Flogger-B* (USSR, 1967): Interceptor. More than 1,000 produced. First Soviet combat aircraft with variable geometry wings. MiG-27 (*Flogger-D*) is ground-attack version. *Span:* 14.2–8.7 m (46 ft–26 ft 9½ in) *Length:* 16.4 m (55 ft 1½ in) *Max speed:* Mach 2.3 *Powerplant:* 1 × Tumansky reheated turbofan, 9,300 kg (20,500 lb) st

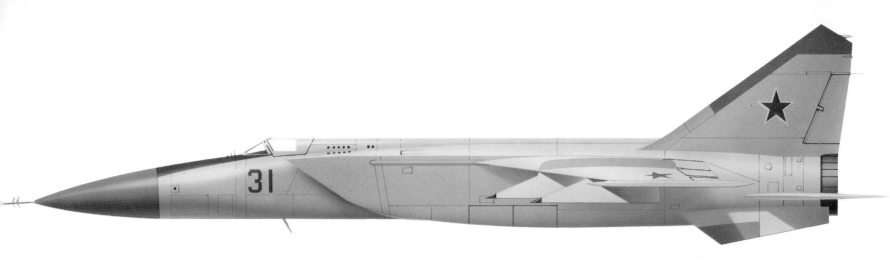

Mikoyan MiG-25 *Foxbat* (USSR, *c* 1964): Very high performance high altitude interceptor and reconnaissance fighter. World's fastest fighter and operational ceiling reportedly in excess of 24,000 m. *Span:* 14.0 m (45 ft 9 in) *Length:* 22.3 m (73 ft 2 in) *Max speed:* Mach 3.0 *Powerplant:* 2 × Tumansky R-266 turbojets, each 11,000 kg (24,250 lb) st with a/b

Sukhoi Su-15 *Flagon* (USSR, 1966): All-weather single-seat-interceptor fighter. Delivery to Soviet air forces started 1969 with production continuing. Manoeuvrability comparable to F-4 Phantom but carries less armament. *Span:* 10.1 m (30 ft 0 in) *Length:* 21.4 m (68 ft 0 in) *Max speed:* Mach 2.4 *Powerplant:* 2 × afterburning turbojets

Panavia Tornado (UK, West Germany & Italy, 1974): Multi-role combat aircraft built in two variants — Interdiction Strike (IDS) and Air Defence Version (ADV). *Span:* 13.90–8.60 m (45 ft 7¼ in–28 ft 2½in) *Length:* 16.70 m (54 ft 9½ in) *Max speed:* Mach 2.1 *Powerplant:* 2 × TurboUnion RB 199-34R-2 turbofans, each 6,577 kg (14,500 lb) st with afterburning

Tornado prototype at Farnborough Air Show (UK), September 1977
300 mm KR f5.6 + ⅓ 1/500

Sepecat Jaguar (UK & France, 1968): Tactical strike fighter. First deliveries to RAF in June 1973. One fuselage and four wing hardpoints carry maximum ordnance load of 4,500 kg (10,000 lb). *Span:* 8.96 m (28 ft 6 in) *Length:* 15.52 m (50 ft 11 in) *Max speed:* Mach 1.6 *Powerplant:* 2 × RR/Turboméca Adour Mk 102 turbofans, each 3,313 kg (7,305 lb) with a/b

Development Jaguar at Paris Air Show, June 1979
300 mm KR f5.6 1/500

Hawker-Siddeley (BAe) Harrier (UK, 1966): World's first V/STOL strike fighter. Pegasus engine is a vectored-thrust turbofan. Sea Harrier maritime version first flew in 1978. AV-8A version is used by USMC. *Span:* 7.70 m (25 ft 3 in) *Length:* 13.91 m (45 ft 6 in) *Max speed:* Mach 0.95 *Powerplant:* 1 × Rolls-Royce Bristol Pegasus Mk 103, 9,752 (21,500 lb) st

Harrier GR.3 at RAF Waddington, June 1979
400 mm KR f5.6 1/500

22

BAC (BAe) Lightning (UK, 1957): Interceptor with vertically superimposed twin engines. Production ended September 1972. *Span:* 10.61 m (34 ft 10 in) *Length:* 16.84 m (55 ft 3 in)

Max speed: Mach 2.27 *Powerplant:* 2 × Rolls-Royce Avon 302-C turbojets, each 7,393 kg (16,300 lb) with afterburning

Lightning F.6 at RAF Valley, May 1978
200 mm KR f5.6 1/500

23

Hawker Siddeley (BAe) Buccaneer (UK, 1958): Strike aircraft designed for carrier-borne low-level cruising and attack. Most Buccaneers were transferred to RAF when relinquished by Royal Navy. *Span:* 13.41 m (44 ft 0 in) *Length:* 19.33 m (63 ft 5 in) *Max speed:* Mach 0.92 *Powerplant:* 2 × Rolls-Royce RB168-1A Spey Mk 101 turbofans, each 5,035 kg (11,100 lb) st

RAF Buccaneer S.2B at RAF Air Tattoo (UK), June 1979 300 mm KR f5.6 1/500

Dassault-Breguet Mirage III (France, 1956): Interceptor and close-support delta-wing light fighter. Developed into ground attack (Mirage 5) and increased-power (Mirage 50) versions.

Total production: 1,300. *Span:* 8.22 mm (27 ft 0 in) *Length:* 15.03 m (49 ft 3½ in) *Max speed:* Mach 2.2 *Powerplant:* 1 × Snecma Atar 9c turbojet, 6,200 kg (13,670 lb) with a/b

Mirage 50 at Paris Air Show, June 1979
300 mm KR f5.6 1/500

Dassault-Breguet Mirage 2000 (France 1978): Lightweight combat fighter with refined delta wing. Will be France's main fighter. *Span:* 9.00 m (29 ft 6 in) *Length:* 15.30 m (50 ft 3½ in) *Max speed:* Mach 2.3 *Powerplant:* 1 × Snecma M53 turbofan, 8,500 kg (18,700 lb) with afterburning

Mirage 2000 prototype at Farnborough Air Show (UK), September 1978
300 mm KR f5.6 + ⅓ 1/500

Dassault-Breguet Super Mirage 4000 (France): Air superiority fighter. Advanced and scaled-up Mirage 2000 with two high-powered engines. Performance data unannounced but reported comparable to F-15 Eagle. *Span:* 12 in (39 ft 4½ in) *Length:* 18.7 m (61 ft 4¼ in) *Powerplant:* 2 × Snecma M53 turbofans, each 8,500 kg (18,700 lb) with a/b

Mirage 4000 at Paris Air Show,
June 1979
400 mm KR f5.6 + ⅓ 1/500

27

Dassault-Breguet Mirage F-1 (France, 1966): Multi-purpose fighter. Currently main fighter of French Air Force. Armament is basically two 30 mm cannon and up to five AAMs with maximum capacity of 4000 kg (8,820 lb) *Span:* 9.60 m (27 ft 6¾ in)

Length: 14.31 m (49 ft 2½ in) *Max speed:* Mach 2.2 *Power-plant:* 1 × Snecma Atar 9k-50 turbojet, 7,200 kg (15,873 lb) st with afterburning.

Mirage F-1E at Farnborough Air Show (UK), September 1978 300 mm KR f5.6 + ⅓ 1/500

Dassault-Breguet Super Etendard (France, 1976): Carrier-based tactical fighter. Redesigned from Etendard IV of late 1950's with increased power and modernised avionics. *Span:* 9.6 m (31 ft 6 in) *Length:* 14.31 m (46 ft 11½ in) *Max speed:* Mach 1.05 *Powerplant:* 1 × Snecma Atar 8k-50 turbojet, 5,110 kg (11,265 lb) st with afterburning

Super Etendard at Paris Air Show, June 1979
300 mm KR f5.6 + ⅓ 1/500

29

SAAB 37 Viggen (Sweden, 1967): Multi-purpose fighter with uniquely designed double-delta wings with good STOL performance, Viggen can take off from standard highway. SF37 and SH37 reconnaissance versions. *Span:* 10.60 m (34 ft 9¼ in) *Length:* 16.30 m (53 ft 5¾ in) *Max speed:* Mach 2.0 *Powerplant:* 1 × Volvo Flygmotor RM8A turbofan, 11,800 kg (26,015 lb) st with afterburning

AJ-37 from SAAB 105, July 1975
80–200 mm zoom KX f8+1 1/250

SAAB 35 Draken (Sweden, 1955): All-weather fighter with compound delta wings. Main frontline fighter of Swedish Air Force. Total production 600, ending in 1972. *Span:* 9.40 m (30 ft 10 in) *Length:* 14.28 m (50 ft 4 in) *Max speed:* Mach 1.6 *Powerplant:* 1 × Volvo Flygmotor RM6C turbojet, 8,000 kg (17,650 lb) st with afterburning

J-35A at Erding AB (Luftwaffe), May 1978
50 mm KM f8+⅓ 1/250

Mitsubishi F-1 (Japan, 1975): Close-support fighter. Japan's first attack fighter since WW2. Developed from T-2 supersonic trainer, is faster and lighter than comparable Jaguar. *Span:*

7.88 m (25 ft 10¼ in) *Length:* 17.85 m (58 ft 6¾ in) *Max speed:* Mach 1.6 *Powerplant:* 2 × Rolls-Royce/Turboméca Adour Mk 804 turbofans, each 3,207 kg (7,070 lb) st with a/b

F-1 at Misawa AB (JASDF), January 1978
200 mm KM F5.6 + ⅔ 1/500

IAI Kfir (Israel, 1971): Tactical attack fighter based on Mirage III but redesigned with increased power and forward canard wing to improve manoeuvrability on Kfir-C2. *Span:* 8.22 m (26 ft 11½ in) *Length:* 15.55 m (51 ft 0¼ in) *Max speed:* Mach 2.29 *Powerplant:* 1 × General Electric J79 turbojet, 8,120 kg (17,900 lb) st with afterburning

Kfir C2 at Paris Air Show, June 1977 300 mm KR f5.6 1/500

FMA IA58 Pucara (Argentina, 1969): Counter-insurgency aircraft with two turboprop engines for light attack and reconnaissance duties. Two 20 mm cannon and four 0.3 in machine guns in forward fuselage. *Span:* 14.50 m (47 ft 6¾ in) *Length:* 14.10 m (46 ft 9 in) *Max speed:* 520 km/h (323 mph) *Powerplant:* 2 × Turboméca Astazou XV19 turboprops, 1,022 ehp

IA58 at Farnborough Air Show (UK), September 1978
300 mm KR f5.6 1/500

Lockheed AC-130 (USA): Gunship modification of C-130 Hercules tactical transport with 105 mm howitzer, 42 mm cannon, two 20 mm rotary cannon, two 7.62 mm Gatlings. *Span:* 40.41 m (132 ft 7 in) *Length:* 29.78 m (97 ft 9 in) *Max speed:* 555 km/h (345 mph) *Powerplant:* 4 × Allison T56-A-15 turboprops, each 4,508 ehp

AC-130A at Eglin AFB (USAF), June 1977
200 mm KR f5.6 + ⅓ 1/500

35

Rockwell International B-1 (USA, 1974): Four-seat strategic bomber and missile platform. Much smaller than B-52, uses extremely advanced efficient engines and high-lift variable-sweep wing. B-1B ordered for USAF. *Span:* 41.67–23.84 m (136 ft 8½ in–78 ft 2½ in) *Length:* 45.78 m (150 ft 2½ in) *Max speed:* Mach 2.0 *Powerplant:* 4 × General Electric YF101-GE-100 turbofans, each 13,600 kg (30,000 lb) st with afterburning

B-1 at Edwards AB (USAF), February 1978
300 mm KR f5.6 + ⅔ 1/500

36

Boeing B-52 Stratofortress (USA, 1952): Long-range strategic bomber planned in 1946, production completed in 1962 and still in front-line service. Work began in 1972 to adapt B-52s in Strategic Air Command inventory to carry eight SRAMs (Short Range Attack Missiles). *Span:* 56.42 m (185 ft 0 in) *Length:* 48.03 m (157 ft 7 in) *Max speed:* Mach 0.95 *Powerplant:* 8 × Pratt & Whitney TF-33-P3 turbofans, each 7,718 kg (17,000 lb) st

B-52G at Mather AFB (USAF), October 1974
200 mm K-II f8 1/125

37

Hawker Siddeley (BAe) Vulcan (UK, 1952): Long-range tactical bomber. Developed to become one of the V-force bombers with which RAF maintained Britain's strategic nuclear deterrent until this task was transferred to Royal Navy's Polaris-equipped submarines. *Span:* 33.83 m (111 ft 0 in) *Length:* 30.45 m (99 ft 11 in) *Max speed:* Mach 0.98 *Power-plant:* 4 × Rolls-Royce Bristol Olympus Mk 301 turbojets, each 9,072 kg (20,000 lb) st

Vulcan B.2 at Abbotsford Air Show (Canada), August 1977

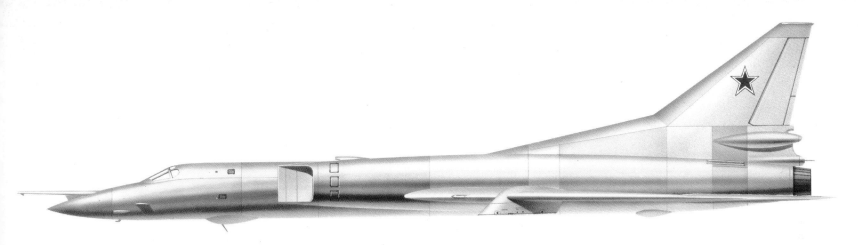

Tupolev Tu-26 *Backfire* (USSR, c 1969): Strategic bomber with variable geometry wings. Development believed begun in mid-1960's. Put into service with Soviet Air Force and Navy in 1975–76. *Span:* 34.50–27.50 m (113 ft–86 ft) *Length:* 40.50 m (132 ft 0 ins) *Max speed:* Mach 2.0 *Powerplant:* 2 × Kuznetsov turbofans, each 20,000 kg (44,090 lb) st

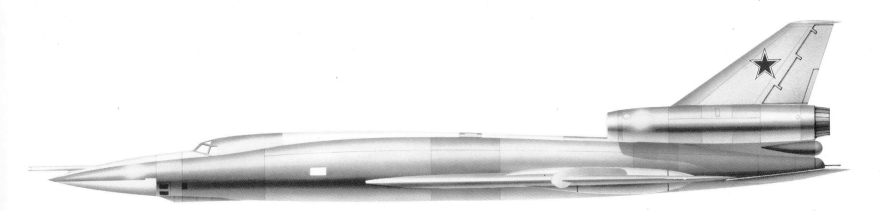

Tupolev Tu-22 *Blinder* (USSR, c 1961): First Soviet supersonic long-range medium bomber. Two high-powered engines mounted below fin. Maritime reconnaissance version also in service. Maximum load about 5000 kg. *Span:* 22.70 m (90 ft 10½ in) *Length:* 40.50 m (132 ft 11½ in) *Max speed:* Mach 1.4 *Powerplant:* 2 × turbojets, each 12,050 kg (27,000 lb) st

Lockheed P-3C Orion (USA, 1958): Long-range patrol aircraft. Packed into the airframe of P-3C advanced version is a new tactical system with sensors and weapons controlled by a digital computer. *Span:* 30.37 m (99 ft 8 in) *Length:* 35 ft 17 m (116 ft 10 in) *Max speed:* 761 km/h (473 mph) *Powerplant:* 4 × Allison T56-A-14 turboprops, each 4,910 ehp

P-3C at Misawa AB (JASDF), January 1978
200 mm KR f5.6 + ⅓ 1/500

Lockheed S-3A Viking (USA, 1972): Carrier-borne anti-submarine aircraft. The operational equipment costs considerably more than the aircraft itself. *Span:* 20.93 m (68 ft 8 in)

Length: 16.26 m (53 ft 4 in) *Max speed:* 834 km/h (518 mph) *Powerplant:* 2 × General Electric TF34-GE-2 turbofans, each 4,207 kg (9,275 lb) st

S-3A from the carrier USS Eisenhower, *August 1978* 300 mm KR f5.6 + ⅓ 1/500

41

Dassault-Breguet Atlantic (France, 1961): Long-range maritime patrol craft. Packs tactical equipment, sonobuoy, torpedoes and anti-submarine missiles in its fuselage. Total production: 20 for W. Germany, 9 for Netherlands, 40 for France, 18 for Italy. *Span:* 36.30 m (119 ft 1 in) *Length:* 31.75 m (104 ft 2 in) *Max speed:* 657 km/h (409 mph) *Powerplant:* 2 × Snecma/Rolls-Royce Tyne R Ty 20 Mk 21 turboprops, each 6,106 ehp

Atlantic in Air Tattoo June 1979
300 mm KR f5.6 1/500

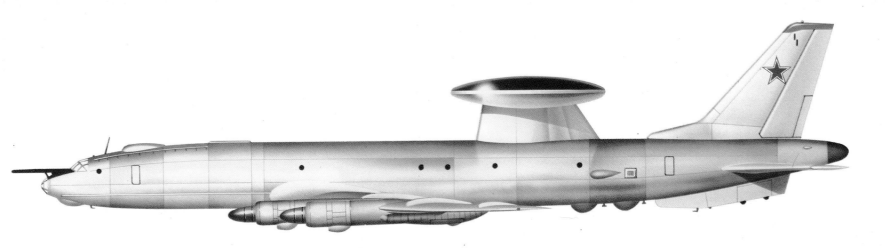

Tupolev Tu-126 *Moss* (USSR *c* 1967): Airborne early warning and control system aircraft. Adaptation of Tu-114 commercial transport. Dominant feature is pylon-mounted-rotating 'saucer' early warning radar. *Span:* 51.2 m (167 ft 8 in) *Length:* 57.3 m (188 ft 0 in) *Max speed:* 815 km/h (460 mph) *Powerplant:* 4 × Kuznetsov NK-12MV turboprops, each 14,795 ehp

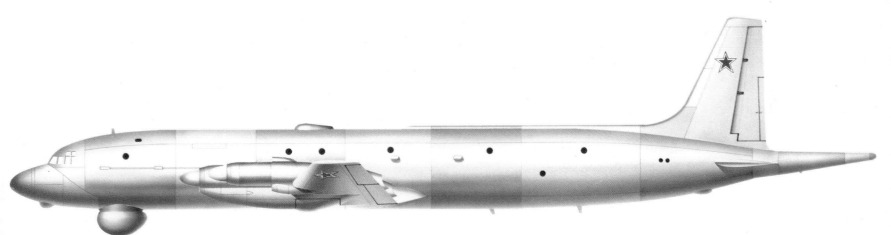

Ilyushin Il-38 *May* (USSR *c* 1971): Long-range maritime patrol aircraft. Evolved from the Il-18 commercial transport somewhat as Lockheed Orion did from Electra airliner. *Span:* 37.4 m (122 ft 8½ in) *Length:* 39.9 m (129 ft 10 in) *Max speed:* 648 km/h (400 mph) *Powerplant:* 4 × Luchenko A1-20M turboprops, each 4,250 ehp

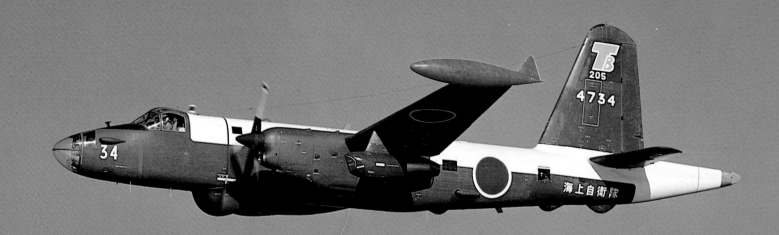

Kawasaki P-2J (Japan, 1966): Maritime and anti-submarine patrol aircraft. Using basically the same wing and tail units as Lockheed P-2 Nepturne, P-2J has a lengthened fuselage to accommodate a more modern search and control system.

Span: 29.78 m (97 ft 8½ in) *Length:* 29.23 m (95 ft 10¾ in) *Max speed:* 556 km/h (350 mph) *Powerplant:* 2 × General Electric T64-IHI-10 turboprops, each 2,850 ehp, 2 × auxiliary turbojets

P-2J from Shimofusa NAS (Japan), January 1979 105 mm KM f5.6 1/250

Shin Meiwa US-1 (Japan, 1967): Long-range patrol and rescue flying-boat. Developed in Japan as new anti-submarine aircraft. Amphibian version is equipped as a rescue unit and known as US-1. *Span:* 32.78 m (108 ft 8¾ in) *Length:* 33.50 m (109 ft 11 in) *Max speed:* 500 km/h (315 mph) *Powerplant:* 4 × General Electric T64-IHI-10 turboprops, each 3,060 ehp

US-1 at Tokyo Aerospace Show, October 1976
400 mm KR f8 + ⅓ 1/250

45

Hawker Siddeley (BAe) Nimrod (UK, 1967): Long-range maritime patrol aircraft designed as replacement for long-serving Shackletons. Derived from Comet airliner with addition of unpressurised pannier under fuselage to accommodate weapons bay and operational equipment. *Span:* 35 m (114 ft 10 in) *Length:* 41.37 m (126 ft 9 in) *Max speed:* 852 km/h (533 mph) *Powerplant:* 4 × Rolls-Royce RB 168-20 Spey Mk 250 turbofans, each 5,506 kg (12,140 lb) st

Nimrod MR.Mk 1 at Kinloss AB (UK), October 1975 35 mm K-II f5.6 1/250

BAe Nimrod AEW (UK, 1978): Airborne Early Warning and control system aircraft. AEW version to be derived from Nimrod with addition of doppler-radar and data processing and com-munication systems. *Span:* 35 m (114 ft 10 in) *Length:* 41.37 m (126 ft 9 in) *Max speed:* 833 km/h (520 mph)

Comet testbed for Nimrod AEW at Farnborough Air Show (UK), September 1978
300 mm KR f5.6 1/500

47

Boeing E-4 (USA, 1973): Airborne command post with crew/staff of 28–60. Carrying national strategic and economic command and decision-making machinery with unjammable communications and capacity to survive even nuclear war. *Span:* 59.64 m (195 ft 8 in) *Length:* 70.51 m (231 ft 4 in) *Max speed:* Mach 0.92 *Powerplant:* 4 × General Electric F103-GE-100 turbofans, each 23,815 kg (52,500 lb) st

E-4A at Andrews AFB (USA), February 1979
105 mm KM f8 1/125

Boeing E-3A (USA, 1972): Airborne warning and control system platform with crew of 17. Derived from Boeing 707-320B. Carries extremely powerful surveillance radar and mass of sensing and data-processing systems. *Span:* 44.42 m (145 ft 9 in) *Length:* 46.61 m (152 ft 11 in) *Max speed:* Mach 0.83 *Powerplant:* 4 × Pratt & Whitney TF33-PW-100 turbofans, each 9,525 kg (21,000 lb) st

E-3A at Paris Air Show, June 1977
400 mm KR f5.6 1/500

49

Grumman E-2 Hawkeye (USA, 1960): Carrier-borne AEW aircraft, the first designed from scratch as Airborne Early Warning surveillance platform. Equipped with long-range radar with scanner rotating six times per minute. *Span:* 25.46 m (80 ft 7 in) 17.55 m (57 ft 7 in) *Max speed:* 582 km/h (360 mph) *Powerplant:* 2 × Allison T56-A-425 turboprops, 4,910 ehp

E-2C on carrier USS Eisenhower, August 1978
105 mm KM f5.6 1/250

Grumman EA-6B Prowler (USA, 1968): Four-seat carrier-based ECM (Electronic Counter Measure) aircraft. Totally redesigned from A-6 Intruder. Entire payload comprised of the most advanced and comprehensive ECM equipment. *Span:* 16.15 m (53 ft 0 in) *Length:* 18.11 m (59 ft 5 in) *Max speed:* Mach 0.79 *Powerplant:* 2 × Pratt & Whitney J52-P-408 turbojets, each 5,080 kg (11,200 lb) st

EA-6B at NAS Miramar (USA), October, 1974
50 mm K-II f8 1/125

Lockheed U-2 (USA, 1958): High-Altitude special-purpose reconnaissance craft. Glider-like wing allows extraordinarily high ceiling of 25,900 m (85,000 ft). Production to be resumed for special reconnaissance version. *Span:* 24.38 m (80 ft 0 in) *Length:* 15.11 m (49 ft 7 in) *Max speed:* Mach 0.8 *Powerplant:* 1 × Pratt & Whitney J75-P-13 turbojet, 7,710 kg (17,000 lb) st *U-2R at Davis-Monthan AB (USAF), October 1974 80–200 mm zoom KX f8 + ½ 1/250*

Lockheed SR-71 (USA, 1964): Long-range strategic recon- naissance aircraft. Based on YF-12 interceptor, redesigned as follow-up to U-2, capable of flying higher and faster than oppos- ition to penetrate hostile airspace on clandestine over-flights.

Span: 16.95 m (55 ft 7 in) *Length:* 37.74 m (107 ft 5 in) *Max speed:* Mach 3.3 *Powerplant:* 2 × Pratt & Whitney JTIID-20B turbojets, each 14,740 kg (32,500 lb) st

SR-71A at Kadena AB (USAF), April 1979 200 mm KR f4 + ⅔ 1/500

North American (Rockwell) RA-5 Vigilante (USA), 1958): Carrier-borne reconnaissance aircraft comprehensively equipped with multiple sensors, including a side-scanning radar under the fuselage. *Span:* 16.15 m (53 ft 0 in) *Length:* 23.11 m (76 ft 7¼ in) *Max speed:* Mach 2.1 *Powerplant:* 2 × General Electric J79-GE-10 turbojets, each 8,118 kg (17,859) st with afterburning

RA-5C at NAS New Orleans (US Navy), October 1978
300 mm KR f8 + ⅓ 1/250

McDonnell Douglas RF-4 Phantom II (USA, 1958): All-weather multi-sensor reconnaissance aircraft. Reconnaissance version of F-4 Phantom with camera, radar, IR line-scan; also available in model for night missions. *Span:* 11.70 m (38 ft 5 in) *Length:* 19.20 m (62 ft 11¾ in) *Max speed:* Mach 2.4 *Powerplant:* 2 × General Electric J79-IHI-17 turbojets, each 8,120 kg (17,900 lb) st with afterburning

RF-4C at Reno Airport, Nevada, February 1979
200 mm KMf4 + ⅔ 1/500

55

Rockwell OV-10 Bronco (USA, 1965): Forward air control, target tug and utility aircraft. Also serves as lightly armed reconnaissance plane. Four 7.62 mm machine guns in sponsons and total combined capacity of 2,080 kg. Gunship version

OV-10D *Span:* 12.19 m (40 ft 0 in) *Length:* 12.12 m (41 ft 7 in) *Max speed:* 425 km/h (281 mph) *Powerplant:* 2 × AiResearch T/6-G-416 turboprops, each 715 ehp

OV-10A in Air Tattoo, June 1979
300 mm KR f5.6 1/500

Grumman OV-1 Mohawk (USA, 1969): Multi-sensor tactical observation and reconnaissance aircraft. Representing a unique type, it is a specially designed battlefield surveillance machine with exceptional STOL capability. *Span:* 14.63 m (48 ft 0 in *Length:* 12.50 m (41 ft 0 in) *Max speed:* 519 km/h (320 mph) *Powerplant:* 2 × Lycoming T53-L-701 turboprops, each 1,400 ehp

US Army OV-1 at Edwards AFB (USAF), October 1977
200 mm KM f5.6 + ⅓ 1/250

57

Embraer EMB-111 Bandeirante (Brazil, 1977): Maritime reconnaissance version of EMB-110 light transport, with radar and searchlights and ASM armament. Used by Brazilian and Chilean navies. *Span:* 15.32 m (50 ft 3 in) *Length:* 14.83 m (49 ft 9 in) *Max speed:* 404 km/h (250 mph) *Powerplant:* 2 × Pratt & Whitney PT6A-34 turboprops, each 750 ehp

EMB-111B at Farnborough Air Show (UK), September 1978 300 mm KR f5.6 + ⅓ 1/500

BAe 748 Coastguarder (UK, 1977): Maritime reconnaissance aircraft derived from Hawker-Siddeley 748 twin-turboprop airliner. Has search radar under fuselage. Span: 29.95 m (98 ft 3 in) *Length:* 23.77m (78 ft 0 in) *Max cruising speed:* 426 km/h (265 mph) *Powerplant:* 2 × Rolls-Royce Dart R Da.12 Mk 301 turboprops, each 3,245 ehp

Coastguarder at Farnborough Air Show (UK), September 1978
200 mm KR f5.6 + ⅓ 1/500

59

Lockheed C-5A Galaxy (USA): Strategic transport, on some counts the world's largest aircraft. Has 'high flotation' landing gear with 28 wheels capable of operating at maximum weight of 348,800 kg from unpaved surface. *Span:* 67.88 m (222 ft 8½ in) *Length:* 75.54 m (247 ft 10 in) *Max speed:* 919 km/h (571 mph) *Max payload:* 100,229 kg (220,967 lb) *Powerplant:* 4 × General Electric TF39-GE-1 turbofans, each 18,850 kg (41,000 lb) st

C-5A at Indian Springs AB (USAF), March 1979 400 mm KR f5.6 + ⅓ 1/500

Lockheed C-141 Starlifter (USA, 1963): MAC's (Military Airlift Command) most numerous strategic transport. Has very useful combination of range and payload. C141B has fuselage stretched up to 52.52 m (168 ft 4 in) *Span:* 48.74 m (159 ft 11 in) *Length:* 44.20 m (145 ft 0 in) *Max speed:* 919 km/h (571 mph) *Max payload:* 31,136 kg (70,847 lb) *Powerplant:* 4 × Pratt & Whitney TF33-P-7 turbofans, each 9,525 kg (21,000 lb) st

C-141A at Palmdale Airport, Calif., November 1978
300 mm KR f8 1/500

61

McDonnell Douglas YC-15 (USA, 1975): Advanced Medium STOL Transport Prototype. Has EBF (Externally Blown Flap). First prototype flown in August 1975 ASMT programme abandoned 1978. *Span:* 33.63 m (110 ft 4 in) *Length:* 37.87 m (124 ft 0 in) *Max speed:* 804 km/h (500 mph) *Max payload:* 12,340 kg *Powerplant:* 4 × Pratt & Whitney JT8D-17 turbofans, each 7,257 kg (16,000 lb) st

YC-15 at Paris Air Show, June 1977

400 mm KR f5.6+ ⅔ 1/500

Boeing YC-14 (USA, 1976): Second USAF Advanced Medium STOL Transport contender utilising the USB (Upper Surface Blowing) concept. First prototype flown August 1976. ASMT programme abandoned 1978. *Span:* 39.32 m (129 ft 0 in) *Length:* 40.13 m (131 ft 8 in) *Max speed:* 811 km/h (506 mph) *Max payload:* 12,250 kg (27,000 lb) *Powerplant:* 2 × General Electric CF6-50D turbofans, 22,680 kg (50,000 lb) st

YC-14 at Paris Air Show, June 1977
400 mm KR f5.6 + ⅔ 1/500

63

Boeing KC-135 Stratotanker (USA, 1956): World's first jet tanker. Introduced new 'flying boom' refuelling system, mounted under rear fuselage. Total fuel capacity is about 26,000 Imperial gallons. *Span:* 39.87 m (130 ft 10 in) *Length:* 41.53 m (136 ft 3 in) *Max speed:* 945 km/h (585 mph) *Power-plant:* 4 × Pratt & Whitney J57-P-59W turbojets, each 6,327 kg (13,750 lb) st

KC-135A at Palmdale Airport, Calif., November 1978
300 mm KR f5.6 + ⅔ 1/500

Lockheed C-130 Hercules (USA, 1954): US Air Force's first turboprop multi-role transport. Has been in production more than 25 years and continues to be ordered. *Span:* 40.41 m (132 ft 7 in) *Length:* 29.78 m (97 ft 9 in) *Max speed:* 621 km/h (348 mph) *Powerplant:* 4 × Allison T56-A-15 turboprops, each 4,508 ehp

DC-130E drone-carrier at Edwards AFB (USAF), February 1978
200 mm KR f5.6 + ⅔ 1/500

Handley Page Victor (UK, 1952:) Flight refuelling tanker. Originally a strategic bomber the K MK 2 Victor is a conversion with aerial refuelling system and deliveries started in 1974. *Span:* 36.58 m (117 ft 0 in) *Length:* 35.02 m (114 ft 11 in) *Max speed:* 1046 km/h (650 mph) *Powerplant:* 4 × Rolls-Royce Conway R Co. 17 Mk 201 turbojets, each 9,344 kg (20,600 lb) st

Victor K.2A of RAF Waddington, June 1977
200 mm KR f5.6 + ⅓ 1/500

Kawasaki C-1 (Japan, 1970): Japan's first large jet-powered medium-range transport. Its quadruple-slotted Fowler flap provides STOL ability. *Span:* 30.60 m (100 ft 4¾ in) *Length:* 29 m (95 ft 1¾ in) *Max speed:* 793 km/h (507 mph) *Max payload:* 11,900 kg (26,235 lb) *Powerplant:* 2 × Pratt & Whitney JT8D-M-9 turbofans, each 6,575 kg (14,500 lb) st

C-1 of Iruma AB (JASDF), November 1978
200 mm KR f5.6 1/500

Aeritalia G-222 (Italy, 1970): General-purpose transport. Original design called for a combination of cruise turboprops and lift jets for V/STOL capability, but only alternative conventional configuration without lift jets was accepted. Used by Italian, Argentine, Libyan and Dubai air forces. *Span:* 28.80 m (94 ft 2 in) *Length:* 22.70 m (74 ft 5½ in) *Max speed:* 539 km/h (335 mph) *Powerplant:* 2 × General Electric T64-GE-P4D turboprops, each 3,400 shp

G-222 at Paris Air Show, June 1977

300 mm KR f5.6 + ⅓ 1/500

De Havilland Canada DHC-5 Buffalo (Canada, 1964): STOL tactical transport. Can be fitted with ACLS (Air Cushion Landing System) based on the ground effect principle. Instead of wheels the aircraft employs a cushion of air enclosed by an inflatable tube beneath the forward fuselage. *Span:* 29.26 m (96 ft 0 in) *Length:* 24.08 m (79 ft 0 in) *Max speed:* 463 km/h (290 mph) *Max payload:* 8,164 kg (18,000 lb) *Powerplant:* 2 × General Electric CT64-820-4 turboprops, each 3,133 ehp

DHC-5D at Farnborough Air Show (UK), September 1978 300 mm KR f8 1/250–500

Ilyushin Il-76 *Candid* (USSR, 1971): Heavy freighter. Two pilots on flight deck and navigator in station in glazed nose. Generally similar in concept to Lockheed C-141A Starlifter. *Span:* 50.50 m (165 ft 8 in) *Length:* 46.59 m (152 ft 10½ in)

Max speed: 800 km/h (529 mph) *Max payload:* 40,370 kg (88,185 lb) *Powerplant:* 4 × Soloviev D-30KP turbofans, each 12,000 kg (26,455 lb) st

IL-76T at Paris Air Show, June 1979

300 mm KR f5.6 1/500

Antonov An-12 *Cub* (USSR, *c* 1959): Medium-range freighter and troop transport. Differs from US/European counterparts in having defensive tail gun position and is currently Soviet Air Force's most widely used transport. *Span:* 38 m (124 ft 8 in) *Length:* 33.1 m (108 ft 7¼ in) *Max speed:* 777 km/h (444 mph) *Powerplant:* 4 × Ivchenko AI-20K turboprops, each 4,000 ehp

An-12 Cub-B at Niigata Airport, Japan, September 200 mm KX f5.6 1/500

71

Transall C-160 (France & West Germany, 1963): Medium-range tactical transport. Serves French, German, Turkish and South African air forces. Production resumed in 1977. *Span:* 40 m (131 ft 3 in) *Length:* 32.40 m (106 ft 3½ in) *Max speed:* 535 km/h (333 mph) *Powerplant:* 2 × Rolls-Royce Tyne RTy.20 Mk 22 turboprops, each 6,100 ehp

C-160F at Paris Air Show, June 1977

300 mm KR f5.6 1/500

Northrop T-38A Talon (USA, 1959): Advanced trainer with full dual controls at two seats in tandem. First production trainer designed specifically to reproduce flying characteristics of operational supersonic aircraft. Production total 1,193. *Span:* 7.70 m (25 ft 3 in) *Length:* 14.13 m (46 ft 4½ in) *Powerplant:* 2 × General Electric J85-GE-5 turbojets, each 1,746 kg (3,850 lb) st with afterburning

T-38A at Edwards AFB (USAF), February 1978
300 mm KR f8 1/500

Cessna T-37 (USA 1954): Basic trainer with dual controls and side-by-side seats. Used by 16 air forces. A-37 is light strike development. *Span:* 10.30 m (33 ft 9⅓ in) *Length:* 8.92 m (29 ft 3 in) *Max speed:* 685 km (425 mph) *Powerplant:* 2 × Continental J69-T-25 turbojets, each 465 kg (1,025 lb) st

T-37C at Air Tattoo, June 1979
300 mm KR f5.6 + ⅓ 1/500

BAe Hawk (UK, 1974): Advanced trainer. Differs from counterpart Alpha Jet in having single but high-powered engine. Attack version for export has maximum combined capacity of 2,567 kg (5,660 lb). *Span:* 9.40 m (30 ft 9¾ in) *Length:* 11.17 m (36 ft 7¾ in) *Max speed:* 991 km/h (620 mph) *Powerplant:* 1 × Rolls-Royce/Turboméca RT. 172-06-11 Adour 151, 2,422 kg (5,340 lb) st

Hawk T.1 of RAF Valley
28 mm KM f5.6 1/500

Dassault-Breguet/Dornier Alpha Jet (France & West Germany, 1973): Two-seat light tactical aircraft and basic and advanced trainer. Advanced trainer for *l'Armée de l'Air* and light tactical strike aircraft for *Luftwaffe*. *Span:* 9.11 m (29 ft 10¾ in) *Length:* 12.29 m (40 ft 3¾ in) *Max speed:* 991 km/h (620 mph) *Powerplant:* 2 × Snecma/Turboméca Lauzac 04-CS turbofans, each 1,345 kg (2,965 lb) st

Alpha Jet at Farnborough Air Show September 1978
200 mm KR f5.6 1/500

Aerospatiale Fouga 90 Super Magister (France, 1978): Basic trainer. Derives from 1950's production Magister trainer with redesigned fuselage and turbofan engine. *Span:* 11.83 m (38 ft 9 in) *Length:* 9.43 m (30 ft 8 in) *Max speed:* 640 km/h (400 mph) *Powerplant:* 2 × Astafan 11G turbofans, each 689 kg (1,520 lb) st (Development ended, 1980)

Super Magister prototype at Paris Air Show, June 1979 300 mm KR f5.6 + ⅓ 1/500

Aermacchi MB339 (Italy, 1976): Basic trainer derived from the best-selling MB326 with redesigned front fuselage and modernised avionics. Veltro II is single seat attack version.

Span: 10.86 (35 ft 7½ in) *Length:* 10.97 m (36 ft 0 in) *Max speed:* (898 km/h (560 mph) *Powerplant:* 1 × Rolls-Royce Viper Mk 632–43 turbojet, 1,814 kg (4,000 lb) st

MB339 at Farnborough Air Show, September 1978
200 mm KR f5.6 1/500

CASA C-101 Aviojet (Spain, 1977): New basic jet trainer and light tactical aircraft planned for economy in production and operation rather than performance. *Span:* 10.60 m (34 ft 9⅜ in) *Length:* 12.25 m (40 ft 2¼ in) *Max speed:* 741 km/h (460 mph) *Powerplant:* 1 × Garrett AiResearch TFE 731-2-25 turbofan, 1,588 kg (3,500 lb) st

C-101 at Farnborough Air Show, September 1978
200 mm KR f5.6 + ⅓ 1/500

Fuji T-1 (Japan, 1958): Japan's first post-war jet trainer. Initial version, T-1A, had imported Orpheus engine. Later T-1B uses indigenous S3 engine. *Span:* 10.49 m (34 ft 5 in) *Length:* 12.12 m (39 ft 9 in) *Powerplant:* 1 × Bristol-Siddeley Orpheus 805 turbojet, 1,814 kg (4,000 lb) st

T-1A at Gifu AB (JASDF), September 1975 200 mm KM f8 1/125

Mitsubishi T-2 (Japan, 1971): Advanced supersonic and combat trainer. Combat training version has 20 mm machine gun on left side of fuselage. Can also carry two AAMs. *Span:* 7.88 m (25 ft 10¼ in) *Length:* 17.85 m (58 ft 6¼ in) *Max speed:* Mach 1.6 *Powerplant:* 2 × Rolls-Royce Turboméca Adour turbofans, each 3,207 kg (7,070 lb) st with afterburning

T-2s of Matsushima AB (JASDF), May 1979
200 mm KR f5.6 + ⅓ 1/500

SIAI Marchetti SF-260 (Italy, 1970): Primary trainer with full dual controls at two side-by-side seats. SF-260 W is light attack version for weapons training and counter-insurgency roles. *Span:* 8.35 m (27 ft 4¾ in) *Length:* 7.10 m (23 ft 3½ in) *Max speed:* 339 km/h (210 mph) *Powerplant:* 1 × Lycoming 0-540-E4A5 piston engine, 260 hp

SF-260W at Paris Air Show, June 1977

300 mm KR f8 + ⅓ 1/250

RFB AWI-2 Fantrainer (West Germany): To be West Germany's basic trainer. AWI-2 prototype has Wankel engine and ducted fan gives jet-like manoeuvrability. *Span:* 9.60 m (31 ft 6 in) *Length:* 8.95 m (29 ft 4¼ in) *Max speed:* 354 km/h (200 mph) *Powerplant:* 2 × Wankel engines, each 150 hp

AWI-2 at Hanover Air Show (West Germany), May 1978
400 mm KR f5.6 + ⅓ 1/500

Sikorsky S-65 H-53 Sea Stallion (USA, 1964): Largest and most powerful helicopter in production outside the Soviet Union. Also as three-engine CH-53E for carrying slung loads up to 18 tons. *Main rotor diameter:* 22.02 m (72 ft 3 in) *Fusel-* *age length:* 26.90 m (88 ft 8 in) *Max speed:* 315 km/h (196 mph) *Powerplant:* 2 × General Electric T64-GE-413 turboshafts, each 3,925 shp

CH-53D at Air Tattoo, June 1979 200 mm KR f5.6 1/500

84

Sikorsky CH-54 Tarhe (USA, 1962): Crane helicopter. Can carry special detachable pod holding up to 45 combat-equipped troops. Only large crane helicopter in the West. *Diameter of six-blade main rotor:* 21.95 m (72 ft 0 in) *Fuselage*

length: 26.97 m (88 ft 3 ins) *Max speed:* 185 km/h (105 mph) *Powerplant:* 2 × Pratt & Whitney T73-P-1 turboshaft, each 4,000 ehp

CH-54B at Fort Lacker (US Army), February 1978
200 mm KR f8 1/250
Rear, Boeing Vertol CH-47C

85

Boeing-Vertol V-107 (USA, 1958): Transport search/rescue, minesweeping helicopter. Boeing built several hundred for US Navy and Marine Corps. The V-107-II is built in Japan under licence by Kawasaki. *Diameter of each main rotor:* 15.54 m (51 ft 0 in) *Fuselage length:* 25.70 m (84 ft 4 in) *Max speed:* 267 km/h (139 mph) *Powerplant:* 2 × General Electric T58-GE-10 turboshafts, each 1,400 shp

KV-107-II-4 at Kisarazu Base (JGSDF), October 1977 300 mm KR f8 + ⅓

Kaman H-2 Seasprite (USA, 1959): All-weather ASW helicopter. Twin-engine Seasprite is assigned to LAMPS (Light Airborne Multi-Purpose System) programme for anti-submarine warfare and shipping strike. *Diameter of main rotor:* 13.41 m (44 ft 0 in) *Fuselage length:* 16.03 m (52 ft 7 in) *Max speed:* 265 km/h (168 mph) *Powerplant:* 2 × General Electric T58-GE-8F turboshafts, each 1,350 shp

SH-2F at NAS Atsugi (JMTSDF),
May 1979
400 mm KR f5.6 1/500

Bell AH-1 HueyCobra (USA, 1965): Two-seat attack helicopter. AH-1G, original Army version, has two 7.62 mm miniguns in the nose turret and rockets or gun pods on the stub wings.

Diameter of main rotor: 13.41 m (44 ft 0 in) *Fuselage length:* 13.54 m (44 ft k5 in) *Max speed:* 352 km/h (219 mph) *Power-plant:* 1 × Lycoming T53-L-13 turboshaft, 1,100 shp

AH-1G at Fort Ruker (US Army), February 1978
105 mm KR f5.6×⅓ 1/500

Bell UH-1 Iroquois (USA, 1956): Fifteen-seat utility helicopter. Developed through many variants. Total production exceeds 6,000. Also produced in Japan, West Germany, Italy and Taiwan. *Diameter of main rotor:* 14.63 m (48 ft 0 in) *Fuselage length:* 17.40 m (57 ft 7 in) *Max speed:* 204 km/h (127 mph) *Powerplant:* 1 × Lycoming T53-L-13 turboshaft 1,400 shp

UH-1H at Fort Ruker (US Army), February 1978
105 mm KR f5.6+⅓ 1/500

89

Aérospatiale SA-330 Puma (Britain, France, 1965): Medium transport helicopter, carries up to 21 equipped troops or 3.2 tons of cargo. Also used by RAF and air arms of France, Portugal, South Africa, Zaïre, Abu Dhabi, Algeria and Ivory Coast. *Diameter of main rotor:* 15 m (49 ft 2½ in) *Length:* 18.15 m (59 ft 6½ in) *Max speed:* 297 km/h (174 mph) *Powerplant:* 2 × Turboméca Turmo IIIC4 turboshafts, each 1,328 shp

Puma CH.1 of RAF Waddington, June 1978

400 mm KR f5.6 + ⅓ 1/500

Westland WG13 Lynx (UK, 1971): Multi-purpose and transport helicopter. Produced in several versions for British Army, Royal Navy and French *Aéronavale* and carries 10 equipped troops or 1.4 tons of cargo. *Diameter of main rotor:* 12.80 m (42 ft 0 in) *Fuselage length:* 15.16 m (49 ft 9 in) *Max speed:* 333 km/h (207 mph) *Powerplant:* 2 × Rolls-Royce Gem turboshafts each 900 shp

Front, Lynx AH.1 at Farnborough Air Show (UK), September 1978 400 mm KR f5.6 1/500 Rear, Sea King HAR.3

Aérospatiale SA-341/342 Gazelle (France/Britain, 1967): Five-seat light utility helicopter with ducted tail fan instead of usual tail rotor. *Diameter of main rotor:* 10.50 m (34 ft 5½ in)

Fuselage length: 9.53 m (31 ft 3¼ in) *Max speed:* 309 km/h (190 mph) *Powerplant:* 1 × Turboméca Astazou IIIA turboshaft, 590 shp

Gazelle HT.3 at Bassingbourn Air Show (UK), June 1978
30 mm KM f5.6 + ⅓

Mil Mi-24 *Hind* D (USSR): Soviet Union's first gunship helicopter. Has rotary cannon in the nose turret and missiles under the stub wings and carries 8–12 equipped troops in the fuselage.

Diameter of main rotor: 17 m (55 ft 9 in) *Max speed:* 333 km/h (201 mph) *Powerplant:* 2 × turboshafts, each 1,500 shp

Mil Mi-12 *Homer* (USSR *c* 1969): Heavy transport helicopter, currently the world's largest. At a weight of 105 tons, the Mi-12 can carry loads of 35 tons. In addition to military uses, has potential for Aeroflot in Siberian logistic support. *Diameter of*

main rotor: 35 m (114 ft 10 in) *Fuselage length:* 37 m (121 ft 4½ in) *Max speed:* 259 km/h (161 mph) *Powerplant:* 4 × Soloviev D-25UF turboshafts, each 6,500 shp

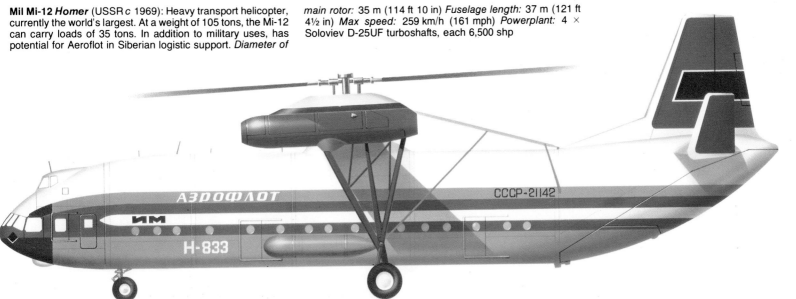

U.S. Navy Fighter
Squadron Badges

VF-1

VF-2

VF-11

Fighter Wing 1

VF-14

VF-24

VF-31

VF-32

VF-33

VF-41

VF-51

VF-84

VF-101

VF-102

VF-111

VF-124

VF-126

VF-142

VF-143

VF-161

VF-202

VF-213

GHOSTRIDERS

VF-301

VF-302

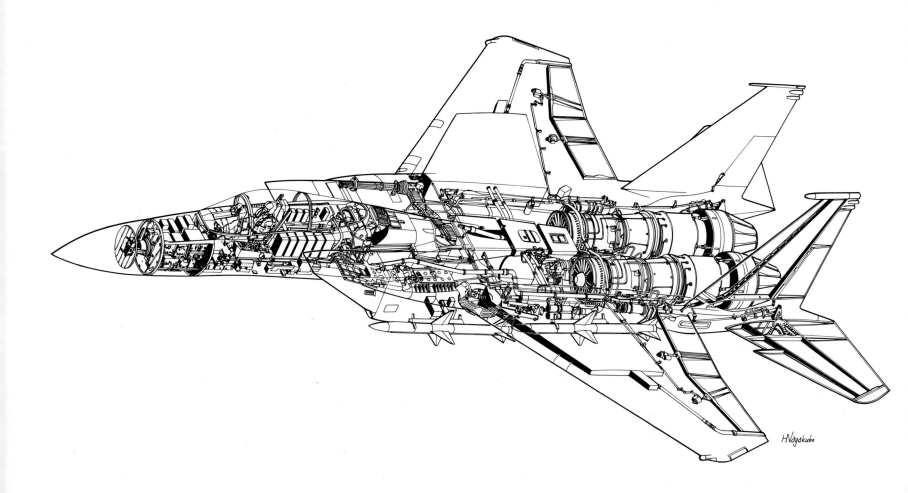

McDonnell Douglas F-15 Eagle